The New Rich

by

Khalid Zidan

SuccessEntrepreneur.org

Get Rich Without Working Yourself to Death

The Secrets of Earning and Accumulating Money Big Time while enjoying the World with Family!

clarifying purposes only and are owned by the owners themselves, not affiliated with this document.

Table of Contents

Chapter 1: How to amass wealth without working yourself to death

"Wealth is the product of industry, ambition, character, and untiring effort."

-Calvin Coolidge

You can be rich, a millionaire, and possibly a billionaire depending on how you handle things.

But even without the millions and billions (maybe that's too far off for you although you're going to get there), your life will never be the same if you earn, say, $50,000 or $100,000 or even more a month.

That's enough money to let you have all the fun, family time, and feasts anytime, anywhere. Unfortunately, not many are doing as well as others – people who believed and acted upon their convictions. You will realize that a simple mind shift could spell the difference. And that's the way to start for you to get rich. My friend, say goodbye to a life of uncertainty. Spend a few minutes perusing this material designed to help you fulfill your dreams, be the person you have always wanted, and start living a life of happiness. Here are the secrets to having this life that you deserve:

Secret #1: Goodbye to Exhaustion + Empty Wallet.

Multi-billionaire Andrew Carnegie, America's second wealthiest man ever, took almost 20 years to make it big. Not only that, he had to work 12 hours a day for many years to make money. Bill Gates worked 16 hours a day to ensure his company would do well, and he is reported to have never had a day off until he turned 31. What was the reason? He wanted to make money and a lot of it.

In Asia, many salarymen, particularly in Japan, suffer from over-exhaustion as they try so hard to make more money. In neighboring China, 600,000 people are reportedly working themselves to death every year. For what again? For MONEY and more of it. Countless others sacrifice rest, sleep, family time, and personal happiness again for extra bucks which disappear like bubbles in an instant.

One need not spend sleepless nights and work hours that are exhausting just to have extra cash. There's an easier and a better way that most people have yet to discover. For them, it simply is next to impossible. But it's NOT.

Why die in your workplace and be enslaved by others when you can be relaxing on a famous beach in the Philippines or cruising on a luxury ship in the Caribbean, sipping your favorite cocktails while earning money? Why not enjoy lazing around your veranda and be embraced by the fresh breeze or wowed by sunsets while your money is multiplying at rates you have never dreamed of before? You can have time with family, travel all year round, play golf, and do a host of other things without worrying about depleting your finances or what would happen to your investments. Is this for real? Absolutely! There are many things about getting rich and making it big that you do not know.

Keep on reading and you'd be amazed at how much you have been missing. And, act fast because every minute lost is worth thousands and thousands of dollars. As they say, time is gold.

Secret #2: You can be rich at 18, not 81.

You can make a lot of money at a young age. Why wait till you're 81 to surround yourself with riches when you can make it big at 18? Learn the secrets of Nick D'Aloisio, Jordan Maron, Ashley Qualls and many others who discovered that people can be financially successful when they are teenagers. Yes, you need not be 30 or 50 or of retirement age to enjoy money and its benefits. This shows you and me that even without education, one can be wealthy. Therefore, if you think that a Ph. D. degree is your road to affluence, think again. There's an easier and faster way.

Secret #3: Tapping the Money-making Machine.

John D. Rockefeller, the wealthiest man who has ever lived, had to go to all the trouble of venturing into all sorts of business to die at 98 years of age with more than $310 billion. You may not be able to beat him, but you certainly have an advantage – you have easy access to technology that he, together with Carnegie and other 20th century entrepreneurs, didn't have the privilege to benefit from. I am talking about the worldwide web – the internet – and the hundreds of social media platforms that can bring money to your doorsteps. I will tell you how you can tap into this money-making machine so that you get to enjoy life while accumulating cash, property, and possessions.

Secret #4: Common sense and lots of courage.

You can be rich by simply having common sense. Indeed, common sense is all about you – what you think about yourself and the world and what actions you take. But common sense is not so common these days that's why many parts of the world are languishing in poverty.

You need to dip your feet in the water to test how deep it is. My point is, you will never enjoy the beauty of the ocean if you simply look at it. Get into the water and check things out. Once in there, you'd see a myriad of colorful sights and shapes hidden from your eyes for the longest time. That's the same as when it comes to making more money. Have you heard about drop shipping? Do you know that you can have your own business with almost no capital at all by employing drop shipping? Has it occurred to you that you can actually use FBA to boost your business or launch a business alone or with a partner?

No one has earned money without common sense, risks and some trial and error. The world can be yours if you only believe. Begin your journey toward financial freedom and wealth unimaginable NOW.

Secret #5: Mindset Change.

To top it all up, you need a change of heart. Others call this a paradigm shift. To accumulate wealth requires a transformation from your inner core. If you take my advice, you can be sure it's just a matter of time before you reach success. I'm certain financial gains will be yours in no time.

Is this for real? Brace yourself, it is.

You've got to believe me, my friend. There are many things about getting rich and making it big that you have yet to discover. And good news, I have them all right here in this book. Keep on reading and you'd be amazed at how much you have been missing. And, act fast because every minute lost is worth thousands and thousands of dollars. As they say, time is gold.

Secret #6: Dispel All Myths About Getting Rich

In relation to secret #5, there are some beliefs you need to bury. It's common for people to believe that getting rich is only for a select few, and not for them, so they choose their lot – to be poor. Others assume that those who have been born with a silver spoon are the only ones who are going to be prosperous in life. In short, you've got to be an heir or an heiress like Paris Hilton to be moneyed. Still for others, reaching the pinnacle of material success is purely a game of luck that if the odds are not against them, they would be affluent somehow, someday.

If you consider these myths, it's obvious that you simply look at yourself as a helpless victim of circumstances and that there's nothing else you can do. You consider yourself unfortunate, confined in a prison that is not of your own making. False and pathetic!

Khalid Zidan

Get rid of these myths if you must have fat bank accounts. Reject such nonsense if you want to join the ranks of the wealthy. Don't give in to resignation if you love yourself and your family. Refuse to embrace fatalism and choose to hurdle the debilitating ideas in your mind. We're living in the 21sth century, and I can be winners, NOW.

You are capable of greatness, of material success. Follow my advice in this e-book and you'd be on the road to victory in no time. I want you to imbibe these truths:

- You can change the way you think and propel yourself to great heights. You were destined for success.

- College or post-graduate education, although essential, is obviously not your key to financial success. When it comes to riches, your greatest resource is discipline.

- Take advantage of the internet, a money-making machine with global reach and unlimited potential. If you're not into online activity, you're living in the medieval times.

- Check all available venues and possibilities to amass wealth. Ask yourself, What are the problems and needs outside my door that I can help solve?

- Above all, keep a little common sense, courage, and risk-taking in your pocket and you'll go a long, long way.

I have good news for you: you can be rich. You can do it.

Chapter 2: Choose Freedom and Financial Prowess

"Wishing will not bring riches. But desiring riches with a state of mind that becomes an obsession, [and] then planning definite ways and means to acquire riches, and backing those plans with persistence which does not recognize failure, will bring riches."

-Napoleon Hill

You read it right – money can and is just within your reach.

Your problem is not lack of opportunities or lack of resources. The real culprit is your inability to know the how and the when, and taking the first step.

If you're clueless, don't worry; I will walk you through this process of experiencing financial success. If you have already started making some strides, I will help you achieve even more. Read on and see how you can make a difference in your life and be financially successful.

Determine Your Direction and Destination

The first step to producing millions is not saving or investing although you will need to do both. The starting point is this: find out what you want to accomplish regarding money and then set goals for yourself. Period.

Believe me, you will not go very far without goals for these are what determine your direction and destination. Yankees legend Yogi Berra aptly said it, "If you don't know where you're going, you'll end up someplace else."

He's right. How many of us end up in wrong places and desperately look for the money? We choose to go to the desert wishing to be able to pan some gold dust instead of mining in the middle of those huge mountains. We rush to the seas and rivers hoping to stumble upon diamonds. If you want to be at the right place at the right time, begin with life and money goals.

Gates' dream was for every American home to have a computer and isn't that the reality now and in many parts of the world? Rockefeller had had a goal to make $100,000 and to reach the age of 100. Perhaps you'd say, I can make that much money in less than a year! Wait before judging the philanthropist. Before underestimating him and his financial goal, you have to realize that such amount of money meant fortunes during his time. Wages during those times were at $.50 a day while a three-month salary was only worth $50.

Now, the question is not whether or not the oil magnate achieved his dreams, but how far he went beyond his target. Indeed, upon his death in 1937, Rockefeller had accumulated a total of $336 billion. He aimed his arrow at Mars, but it ended up in Eris. Did the man live at 100? Well, almost, because he was 98 when he passed away.

Many books on money and financial freedom seldom highlight the importance of having goals. Their view is short-sighted. They forget that the key to earning all the money you want is not by plunging into all the venues for generating cash. They don't emphasize that the starting point is to scribble your life's goals. Without a direction, you'll never achieve anything, for like a ship without a pre-determined course, you would end up broke and a failure. Don't choose failure. Choose success. These thoughts bring us to the next step which is equally important.

Dwell on What You Want

Dreams. Goals. Desires. Plans. Other people call these visions and in their heart of hearts, they are a reality. They can see the future. Edison saw a light bulb and a phonograph, Alexander Graham Bell a telephone, Henry Ford vehicle mass production, Tim Berners-Lee the worldwide web, and the list could go on and on. These guys had one thing in common: they had a vision. To realize their visions, they began the entire process by setting goals and how to reach those goals.

For many extremely successful individuals, dreams are their reality. They transform what they see in their minds into something concrete. When Apple's wizard Steve Jobs floated his idea of producing a mouse to speed up work in the use of computers, he was frowned upon, but he held on to his dream. He never let go of it until a mouse was born.

You and I need to be like these dreamers. Dream, set goals and work on them. Let me reiterate, get rich by having ambitions and being obsessed by them. Be consumed by your dreams until you make them into reality. Speaking of actualizing goals, I think of another word, FOCUS. When you focus on your goal of making money, you work at it, and the result is, of course, money.

You see, money is just the result. But to have the wealth, there is a different path to take. For some it may take a little longer to achieve their goal for many for the road may be bumpy, but for the rest, it may take a little faster because of focus and because of starting right.

You can accumulate a lot of money, and you can it now. But be sure you begin right. After setting those goals, be obsessed by them. Before you know it, you'd be doing something or producing something that you like, and your reward is fulfillment, and of course MONEY and influence. Who would not like both?

Delight in Dreaming Big

Have goals, and be obsessed by them – that's the start. But wait, that's not all. Bill Gates, Steve Jobs, and Rockefeller set goals for themselves, and when they did so, they made sure they kept dreaming for more, for greater things. For them, sky's the limit. That's the attitude all of us must have.

Those who amazingly did very well in amassing wealth not only had definite plans to be successful but they also never stopped aiming for more. And when they dreamt, they dreamt HUGE, as in super big. Theirs was something greater than themselves and beyond their imagination like the first airplane, machine gun, and armored tank conceived of by Da Vinci, who was centuries ahead of his time.

It is often said that big dreams start with small ones. That's right, but the problem with most people is that they may have ambitions, but they let their dreams fossilize and eventually die. The dreams are never nurtured. If you're nearing your goals or if you think you have already achieved them, don't stop the race. Instead, tell yourself it's time to run for another lap. Set higher and much greater goals. You've got to believe there's more to accomplish or achieve.

Every ceiling reached, advises Aldous Huxley, must serve as a floor to the next, much like climbing a ladder or a staircase. After securing a $4,000 capital for a business partnership, Rockefeller went on to dream big by venturing into wholesaling and later on, oil refinery. When that was almost achieved, he went on to make his dream larger. Gates did the same thing. Before he could write the BASIC computer language, he had already dreamt that it would be in the offing and soon he was able to produce it. He announced his Windows (it was only just an idea, an obsession in his head then) even before it became a reality. By the time he turned 31, he had acquired a billion dollars, and you guessed it right, from Windows, which he had earlier envisioned. And the rest is history, as it's often said.

Technology innovator Steve Jobs, at first, set goals of producing something out of his step-father's garage; but he knew he was meant for something great in this world. True enough, he was able to establish Apple that would do away with the bulky desktop screens and replace them with slim ones thanks to this genius who was not at all a computer programmer. His next dream was to enable technology users to hold the internet in their hands, and that led to the invention of his celebrated iPad.

Some people are exceptional at having visions and articulating their dreams, but they are terrible when it comes to sustaining those ambitions. It's one thing to have plans, but it's another thing to execute them. To make money, you must actualize your vision and goals. One thing is sure: money will not come knocking at your doorstep without a clear direction. You chase the money; look for it.

Have you ever wondered how Alaska supplies fuel to the rest of the American states? It's through a pipeline called Trans-Alaska Pipeline System that brings oil to where it should go. You need to do the same – actualize your dreams by building your pipeline. And once it's constructed, money would start coming. In short, know your destination and the prize you want, secure your path and start running the race.

You can be Wealthy without Education & Experience

Training and education are good, but you can be wealthy without them. There's no guarantee that if you accumulate all the knowledge you want in the world, you will end up financially successful. In fact, The Atlantic has reported that a staggering 60% of people with doctoral degrees and more than 80% of individuals with life science PhDs end up being jobless after graduation. Since what fuels the world is money, you have to start setting goals on accumulating wealth at what speed and how much at a particular timeframe. Then pursue your other dreams later on, including your desire for education.

Famous millionaires Mark Zuckerberg, founder of Facebook, together with Bill Gates, and Steve Jobs did not even have college diplomas! Gates and Zuckerberg dropped out of Harvard while Jobs did not finish his studies at Reed College. Look where these people are now. All three join the ranks of Star Wars'James Cameron, famous actor Tom Hanks, singer Lady Gaga, and millionaire TV host and actress Oprah Winfrey to name just a few. Even the greatest multibillionaires - Carnegie and Rockefeller – did not have enough education, yet they built up wealth more than one could ever imagine.

What do these men and women have in common? FAITH. They all believed. They saw the future and made that future happen to their advantage. What they imagined would, later on, become a reality. Theirs was the assurance, the confidence that what they had hoped for could become a real. You can be like them if you focus on your direction and destination and then journey with dedication.

Drive, Dedication, and Hard work

The pipeline principle is connected to this next requirement on how to start making more money. Learn from Jack Ma, the CEO of Alibaba and the richest man in China. His company is reportedly worth $231 billion, and the former English teacher himself is worth more than $19 billion, one of the richest in the world. What is his secret? Simple: drive and dedication. Hold on a second, I don't intend to go that far, you might say. But the principle is the same: if you want to make it big, maybe start earning double or triple than what you're getting now, you must be driven. Sprinkle some dedication and hard work and boy, you'd see amazing results. I know some people who are naturally hard working, but they fail to hit the jackpot. The problem is, there's no diligence, no discipline, no motivation.

When one is driven and dedicated, no amount of failure will stop them. Possessing the minds of such inventors as Thomas Alva Edison, who perfected the light bulb after 1,000 unsuccessful attempts, they will not give up until they produce the results they expect. When one is dedicated, they also work hard. They exert more effort, because, in the first place, they are driven. How can one be driven when their problem emanates from their very core? It's one thing to come up with a set of goals, but it's another thing to work on them. Some people are good at the thinking part, but not the doing aspect.

Now, here's one of the most critical strategies for financial success: heart "surgery". Read the next chapter and find out how changing your perspective spells all the difference in being financially successful.

Chapter 3: How changing your mindset can make you rich

"The highest purpose of intellectual cultivation is to give a man a perfect knowledge and mastery of his own inner self; to render our consciousness its own light and its own mirror."

-Frederich Leopold von Hardenber

The Pythagoreans, according to Dr. Isaac Watts, had a very sacred rule in life. It was their practice to evaluate all the day's activities or events before going to sleep. The evaluation was not done only once or twice but thrice. The reason, of course, is obvious – they wanted to ascertain how they fared in all their affairs, what was done wrong and what was accomplished right. Presumably, they also checked their attitudes and motives in all their endeavors. Did they have the right heart? Where they guided by noble goals? Did they believe?

Like the Pythagoreans, all of us need to evaluate our lives from time to time because doing so is a critical step towards financial success. To be wealthy, you need to look inward first. Yes, begin with an honest look at yourself. Looking inward allows you to understand your need to undergo a heart surgery, even a brain surgery. The point is this: making money is all about psychology. To accumulate wealth, you have to have a brand new mind, convinced that everything is possible to those who believe. According to Equity Group

Investments founder Sam Zell, the state of one's mind dictates his or her lot in life, particularly the area of financial stability. In an interview, Zell said, "Why is it always assumed that somebody doesn't succeed because he can't, as opposed to he doesn't want to...?" In short, Zell is arguing that people are poor because they choose to be poor. It's not that they are helpless, but because they don't try. I agree a hundred percent.

Indeed, an inner overhaul must take place if you have to start making lots of money. Your whole being must undergo a psychological MRI and pinpoint those thoughts that tell you that it is simply impossible to be rich. Things inside of you must be recalibrated. No, it's more than just embracing the power of positive thinking, although that is a necessary ingredient. It's about unlearning things and doing away with negativism, skepticism, resignation, and even fatalistic tendencies. Believe in yourself that you can succeed. Stop blaming others and circumstances. You need the minds and hearts of such men like Edison, Rockefeller, Carnegie, Gates, Jobs, Ma and many more if you want to be successful financially.

Secrets of Having a New Heart and a New Mind

Dr. Raghavendra Gowda, Chairman & Managing Director of the London-based Shree Balajee Group, believes that negative thoughts can "quickly creep" into one's life. However, he is convinced that every man and woman is capable of overcoming such thoughts and replacing them with good ones.

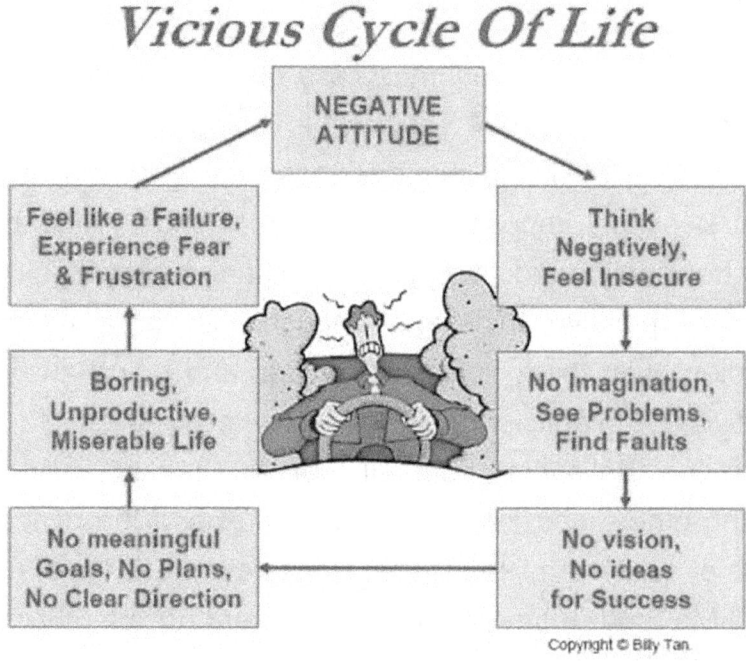

Vicious Cycle Of Life

Copyright © Billy Tan.

Gowda, citing Billy Tan's "Vicious Cycle of Life" concept, highlighted how negative attitudes can dictate the quality of life of a person. Based on Tan's paradigm, if we maintain negative attitudes, we subject ourselves to a life of misery. As we nurture negative attitudes, we end up harboring negative thoughts as well as of feelings of insecurity. Such a state of mind leads to a number of things: a lack of imagination and a tendency to see problems and find faults in others.

To amplify Tan, I suppose negativism can also lead us to think faultily of ourselves and of life in general. Because we are saturated by all the negative vibes, our perspectives become clouded, resulting in the lack of vision. When we don't see the future, we get stuck in the day-to-day grind, with no meaningful goals and plans. That means a life without clear direction. Every day, then, becomes a bore, and we also end up being unproductive and miserable. The cycle leads to a feeling of being a failure which generates more negative thoughts and emotions, according to Tan. Indeed, a vicious cycle of life! Don't be caught in it. And if you have already been trapped, you can still be free! Let me give you tips toward freedom that leads you to achieve your money goals, among others.

1. Do a Self-evaluation

I referred to this earlier as mind and heart surgery, an inner overhaul. Be sure to follow the following steps:

- Identify Wrong Attitudes and Beliefs. Go to a quiet place, sit down and conduct a thorough check of what you have believed all this time. Find out if you have any negative thoughts about yourself and your life. Get a pen and paper and list them down. Resist the temptation that it will be difficult, or it's going to be a waste of time. It will be worth it. Remember, it's about your life, where you're headed. You deserve this much-needed self-appraisal and evaluation.

- Ask others of their appraisal of you. Talk to a friend, a relative or a co-worker and ask them what sort of things they know or see about you – both positive and negative. Give yourself a tap on the back for everything positive about you, but think through all their honest comments. Pay particular attention to your set of beliefs, attitudes, and perspectives that often lead to skepticism and negativism.

- Get rid of negative thoughts. Once you've identified all the negative thoughts about yourself, your life and financial future, throw them out of the window. They don't deserve a space in your life. Concentrate on the good things about you and believe that you can achieve your money goals. Of course, try to overcome the not-so-good in you because they can get in the way.

- Transform your mind. It's not enough to know what debilitating thoughts have been overwhelming you. It is important for you to get rid of them. But don't stop there. You must replace them with good and new ones. Act now before it's too late. A famous saying goes,

"Plant a thought and reap a word;
plant a word and reap an action;
plant an action and reap a habit;
plant a habit and reap a character;
plant a character and reap a destiny."

There's only one culprit if one is in a miserable lot or if they lack financial resources – the mind. Begin changing your thoughts before they begin changing you.

- Claim and actualize newly acquired thoughts. Teach yourself to think only of what is noble, right, true, and lovely about yourself and your financial prowess. Believe that all is yours, and then think of them often. Write down the things you want to achieve and declare that they are going to be yours.

Here is a sample list:

a) I am capable of doing great things.

b) I am not a helpless victim of circumstances and poverty.

c) I have talents and skills. I am gifted.

d) I can reach my full potential.

e) I can tap these inner resources to be financially successful.

f) I will be out of debt in 2 years.

g) I will be a millionaire in 3 years time.

The list can go on and on. Start imagining good things about yourself and the future. Imagine a big house, a brand new car, fast cash in the back, a cruise in Mediterranean, and so on. Have a can-do attitude and you'd see the difference.

2. Possess I CAN Mindset

If others were able to do it, why can't you? Every day, according to Christopher Rice, is like a bank account, and time is everyone's currency. All are equal and endowed with a similar resource which is time. Whoever we are, whether we're a royalty or simple people, whether heirs to fortunes or possessing no property at all – we have an essential commodity. Each is given time and has 24 hours a day to think, plan, and work on how to get rich. Many people who have become millionaires and billionaires did not have more time than others. No, their strategy was to take advantage of the same 24 hours, thinking and processing how they could become successful. They dwelt on the I CAN mindset and were driven by that same determination. They never gave up until they succeeded.

American industrialist Henry Ford had this to say, "Whether you think you can, or you think you can't – you're right." In short, we do not succeed and make money as we should because many of us have resolved that it is simply difficult if not impossible. If one is not motivated, they will not be driven to work hard and pursue the dreams or the goals they have set. But, if they are obsessed with something they'd like to achieve, they will maintain a singular mindset: I can get what I want. I can be rich in no time.

The secret to making money? Attitude. This is your launching pad, the place for takeoff. All the other strategies will depend largely on your state of mind.

3. Avoid Passivity: Start helping yourself

What is the cause of poverty? Here's the answer: people are not helping themselves. And why are people passive? It is because they are not convinced they can change their lot in life.

According to a study conducted by the US National Public Radio, in collaboration with the Kaiser Family Foundation and the Harvard University's Kennedy School, 48% of those polled believed poverty is a result of people's failure to help themselves. Those surveyed (a total of 2000 individuals) were 18 years old and above and consisted of random respondents. You will realize that this is more than just mere laziness. It is more of motivation issue, of lack of faith in oneself and the possibility of a better life.

Some people simply do not have the will to improve their plight in life. In the same poll, those who were well-off indicated the same conclusion, with 50% of them stating that the poor were not helping themselves. This perception was also shared by 39% of the respondents coming from a poor background. The study concluded that people are penniless because they do not have the aspirations to make it big while others do not believe in hard work. It's not part of their agenda or life goals.

Here's your action point: Change the way you think. A famous Portuguese proverb aptly puts it, "Change yourself and fortune will change with you." Therefore, resolve to have goals, to work on those goals, be obsessed by those goals, keep dreaming big, and plan on getting rich. As someone has said, if we don't plan to succeed, we plan to fail.

Therefore, if you do not decide to get rich, you choose to get poor.

All you need to do is believe that in this world there are lots of opportunities for every individual to take advantage of, but we need to act by having ambitions and making them happen. Do so with enough drive and dedication. The rest of the ingredients of success are just going to be the automatic outcomes or offshoot.

What are these results? These opportunities? Where do I begin? Answers are found in the next section of the e-book.

Chapter 4: Don't be a slave for life, be your own boss

"I think earning money is the simplest thing in the world once you learn how to do it. It's like driving a car. It's simple if you know how to do it."

-Bob Proctor

Believing in yourself, your talents and your skills is the starting point to getting rich. Alongside this change of mindset is the need to start setting goals both for the short and long haul. Once set, focus on them and work on them. This is what we mean by helping yourself.

The key to accumulating wealth is working on your dreams. There's no magic. Luck is not even a factor. You determine your future. I have made this very clear. Where do you go from here? Be your own boss – start your own business or businesses. How? Do any or all of the following:

1. Use Your Talents and Skills

After looking inward and changing your mindset, it's time to consider your talents and skills. Think of what you are capable of doing and/or producing, something that can generate income. Can you produce bread, cakes, home and office supplies, electronic products, gadgets, etc.? After Japan had been destroyed by two powerful bombs during World War II, it concentrated on developing technology with the war compensation from the United States, a move that transformed the Asian country into one of the wealthiest nations in the world. The Japanese relied on their ingenuity, and they were able to propel themselves to greatness.

Learn from the Japanese. The secret here is that you must determine what you are capable of doing and/or producing that can generate income. Again, use your talents and skills. In particular, think of goods and services that can be sold or offered to prospective customers. Start your marketing in your community with the intent of expanding beyond your borders. Whether you are employed or not, you must realize that this is one of the best routes towards financial success.

Production does not always mean invention. You can improve on something that has already been there. It is said that before pizza was invented, Italian immigrants in New York wasted lots leftover bread until a smart and ingenious mother recycled them. After gathering all the leftovers, she spread some tomato sauce, meat, and cheese, and then put them in a pan and heated them in the oven for a few minutes. And voila the precursor of the modern pizza!

2. Have an Entrepreneurial Spirit

Related to the above secret is the need to engage in entrepreneurship. Do more than producing and selling; be one whose intent is to consistently reach markets for your products and services. Did you get the equation? It's think-produce-then-sell proposition. Again, you go back to having a change of heart, of having goals, and then using your talents to produce and sell.

All over the world, you would always find a Chinatown in a major city. If you're observant like me, you've probably noticed something typical in those vibrant enclaves is an entrepreneurial spirit. Cluttered along the usually crowded streets are countless shops – big and small – selling all kinds of stuff. The Chinese believe so much in the value selling. They know that in order to make money, one has to sell goods. Do the same if you want to get rich.

You can't always make a product or offer your own services, but you can still be an entrepreneur. You can move goods produced by others at a higher price, a strategy called buy and sell. Company X manufactures the products and all you do is a market or sell them.

What if you do not have enough capital? Do not worry; you can still be the master of your destiny. How this can be done will be the subject of the discussion in the next chapter.

3. Create a Need or Solve a Problem

Advertisers are brilliant when it comes to creating needs. They introduce a product and tell you it's a needed commodity or service, and we bite on it. Not long ago, everybody washed their dirty plates and pans by hand, but now dishwashers are commonplace. Before McDonald's perfected the fast food system, people prepared food from scratch.

Look around you, what else is not yet being done that you can do? What goods are not being sold? What do people need that is yet to be met by entrepreneurs? What services are lacking? Identify the problems in your city or state and find a way to find a solution. Benjamin Franklin was never idle during his time. He always found ways to address the problems around him. That attitude turned him into of the greatest inventors in the world. Before Google was born, surfing the internet had been a pain in the neck – it took a lot of time. Larry Page saw the problem and thought of coming up with a search engine that had different features, easier to use, and faster to bring internet surfers to their preferred sites. Identifying a need not only helped global internet users but also catapulted the computer scientist to greatness. He became extremely wealthy for solving a problem. His net worth is now valued at $36.2 billion.

Chapter 5: Tapping the money-making machine "The Internet"

"You can't – or you don't want to? I'll accept the second. It's quite possible that you don't want to. It's possible that making this commitment is too scary or too much work…Perhaps you don't want to because it feels financially irresponsible. I think that's an error of judgment on your part,…Turn your passion into money."

-Seth Godi

I was once told a story of a naughty boy who wanted to test the wits of a wise, old woman in a village in India. The woman had always been able to answer every question, so this chap thought of a plan to trap her. He brought a bird and held it behind his back. Then this pal asked the old lady to determine whether the fowl was dead or alive. She began thinking about the question. If she said the bird was alive, the lad would simply have to twist its neck and show her a lifeless bird. If she said the fowl was dead, the boy would show a flapping bird. Instead of answering yes or no, the wise woman came up with an apt reply. She retorted, "the answer is in your hands". What is the moral? You have something in your hands that can change the world and yourself. You've got to use the internet and start generating money from it. You can earn a lot of money via the internet. How?

Mark Zuckerberg made a fortune out of the internet for creating Facebook, which boasts of almost 1.6 billion users (as of the last quarter of 2015), earning himself at least $27 billion worth of shares of the company. Nick D'Aloisio, Jordan Maron, Ashley Qualls, Cameron Johnson, and Robert Nay are some of the many young entrepreneurs who have made it big by tapping this money-making wonder. Let me share at least ten ways to get rich via the internet.

1. Develop an app

If you're into technology such as a mobile app, you're not far from getting rich. Nick D'Aloisio was 15 years old when he developed an app called Trimit, which condenses articles into shorter versions. With support from a billionaire, he came up with a better version called Summly which was reportedly sold to Yahoo for a total of $30 million.

2. Create videos on Youtube

Be like Jordan Maron. Jordan has been one of the most famous YouTube stars because of his CaptainSparklez channel. Through this channel, Jordan posts his Minecraft play videos and song parodies. With millions of subscribers and billions of views, he is reported to have earned at least $8.2 million so far.

3. Internet Design and Advertising

Another money-making business online is designing networking site pages of other people. This is what Ashley

Qualls decided to do. Despite her limited knowledge of HTML, Ashley introduced WhateverLife.com to his network of friends, promoting her design work. As her personalized layouts for people's MySpace pages became more and more popular, she joined Google Adsense, which paid her lots money from advertising revenue. She currently earns millions of dollars via the same online enterprise. Another online business to consider is internet advertising. Cameron Johnson, for example, receives $400,000 a month from an internet advertising venture called SurfingPrizes.com.

4. Introduce Online Games

With no coding experience, Robert Nay taught himself how to make an online game called Bubble Ball which he made available via Apple. With over a million downloads in just over two weeks, his Bubble Ball app dislodged the then favorite Angry Birds game, earning close to $2 million in less than two weeks.

5. Sell Websites

Another way to make money online is by selling web domains. When he was just a teenager, Chris Philips realized that sites would be in demand and so he established his own hosting site. In just less than two years, he was able to earn more than one million US dollars.

6. Selling Miscellaneous items

E-commerce king Jeff Bezos used to take home a six-digit salary, but his passion was telling him to do something else using the internet. After recognizing the potential of selling books online, he went on to launch a company called Amazon.com in 1994. His online bookstore became the model for how online businesses should be operated and racked up sales of more than $610 million plus global customers of 13 million. It is reported that Amazon sells more 200 million products in the United States alone, aside from books. Things that are for sale include clothes, sports and outdoors items, jewelry, electronics, beauty products, baby products, grocery items, and a lot more.

7. Internet Publishing and Blogging

Michael Akinlabi, the author of How to Build an Online Money-Making Machine, highlights the great potential of the internet when it comes to money. He tells of an unsuccessful writer who went on to make more than $2 million dollars in less than two years. The writer's name is Amanda Hocking, a novelist who used the internet to publish her works, according to Akinlabi. The whole point here is taking advantage of the internet to accumulate wealth. He also believes that starting a blog would be a sure way to tap this money-making machine for your own advantage, and I agree. Many people use blogging for their myriads of articles which many internet users read and download for various purposes. Constant and continuous access to the blog site means more traffic, and more internet traffic means advertisements and ad revenues.

8. Freelance Writing and Web Design

Countless individuals earn millions of dollars combined by doing what they love – online writing. There are many famous freelance companies, and these include Upwork Global (formerly oDesk.com) and Freelancers.com. These organizations offer both newbie and professional writers the opportunity to write for global clients composed of companies and individuals. Some of the available jobs are web content writing, copywriting, creative writing, e-book ghostwriting, public relations writing, academic writing, business proposals, grant writing, and much more. Freelance websites are also frequently visited by companies and individuals looking for web designers, graphic artists, and other IT practitioners. If you are a writer or an IT expert, you have a resource with marvelous and endless potential - the internet, offering you countless jobs and other possibilities for you to earn a lot of money.

9. Drop Shipping

If you are by nature an entrepreneur, this one should come easy. Drop shipping has been becoming a more popular way of moving goods from a supplier to the customer. Take note, you don't keep a stock of the goods; you merely promote them in your platform. When orders come, you contact the supplier, and they do the delivery. That's how you earn money in the process with just a little capital involved.

10. Fulfillment By Amazon

Similar to Drop Shipping is FBA or Fulfillment by Amazon. In this internet venture, you deal directly with Amazon to fulfill a delivery. All you do is market the products and let Amazon handle everything – from packaging to delivery. In addition, Amazon takes care of customer service and product returns, which means fewer hassles for you.

These are some of the ways by which you can get rich via the internet, and there are a lot more to discover. The key word here is passion. Together with your passion is a little common sense and lots of courage. The result is a financial success.

Bonus

I have written a blog about the best and quickest 3 ways to earn your first $1,000 in 30 days at http://successentrepreneur.org/how-to-earn-money-from-internet. Let me know what you think in a comment there.

My other books

Blogging for Beginners

http://www.amazon.com/Blogging-Beginners-Successful-Creatives-Business-ebook/dp/B01DR1IARI

New Social Network Platforms in 2016

http://www.amazon.com/Social-Media-Strategy-Platforms-marketers-ebook/dp/B01EJ86IX6

Thank You

If you enjoy the book and bonus, please leave an Amazon review, it takes only 9 seconds :)

www.ingramcontent.com/pod-product-compliance
Lightning Source LLC
Chambersburg PA
CBHW070421190526
45169CB00003B/1353